wildflowers
around the year

photographs and text by **Hope Ryden**

Clarion Books ▪ New York

◉ For Evelyn, who loves and knows the wildflowers ◉

Clarion Books
a Houghton Mifflin Company imprint
215 Park Avenue South, New York, NY 10003
Copyright © 2001 by Hope Ryden

Diagram on page iv by Jessica Battaini.

The text was set in 13-point Joanna.

www.houghtonmifflinbooks.com

Printed in Singapore.

Library of Congress Cataloging-in-Publication Data

Ryden, Hope.
Wildflowers around the year : by Hope Ryden
Includes bibliographical references.
ISBN 0-395-85814-3
1. Wildflowers—Identification—Juvenile literature.
2. Wildflowers—Pictorial works—Juvenile literature.
[1. Wildflowers.] I. Title.
QK117.R93 2001
582.13'0974—dc21   00-043011

TWP 10 9 8 7 6 5 4 3 2

CONTENTS

INTRODUCTION

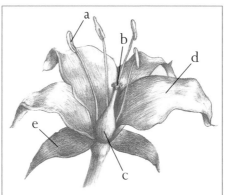

STAMEN male } (a) anther (holds pollen)

PISTIL female } (b) stigma, (c) ovary

(d) petal, (e) sepal

Everyone loves wild-flowers. Wildflowers are so surprising. They appear unexpectedly—unplanted and untended—poking their impudent faces through cracks in side-walks or adding patches of gay color to sun-bleached roadsides and vacant lots. They invade lawns. They brighten dark forests and shady stream banks. Wildflowers are nature's gorgeous jewels, strewn carelessly, willy-nilly, throughout cities and country-sides.

What is a wildflower? Does it exist just to delight our senses? Or does its fragrance and beauty serve some other purpose? Has it a secret life of its own?

Each flower you will meet in this book has a story to tell. Each has evolved strategies that enable it to survive and reproduce itself. To this end, a flower must enlist helpers, for all plants are rooted, unable to move about and mate with oth-ers of their kind, unable to carry their seeds to suitable places.

Who are these helpers? Most flower species de-pend on birds and in-sects to transport their pollen from blossom to blossom, thus enabling them to make seeds. They attract these winged carriers by offering tempting drinks of sweet-tasting nectar located deep inside their blossoms. When a bee or a hummingbird probes for this delicious liquid, it becomes sprinkled with pollen, which it sheds on the next flower it visits. Each flower has developed a way to gain the attention of whatever birds and bees might be in the area. Some do this by a brilliant display of colored petals—red, orange, yellow, blue, or purple. Others simply release an appealing scent.

Of course, human beings, as well as insects, are attracted by sweet smells and bright colors, and many people pick and dig up wildflowers without realizing the harm they are doing. Most wildflowers wilt before they can be placed in a vase, and only a few "take" when transplanted to a garden spot. Since many species are becoming rare and even endangered, it makes sense to leave wildflowers where they have come up on their own. That is where they do best, and that is where they look best. Just finding them in their secret haunts is a pleasure in itself and can be turned into an interesting and challenging hobby.

This book is my record of such a year-long pursuit. If you enjoy treasure hunts, you might do the same thing.

You are bound to find wildflowers that aren't included in this book, for there are more than 250,000 known species in the world! Why not make notes or drawings about the wildflowers you discover and create a journal of your own? A nearby park or meadow or stream will provide a change of scene every time you visit it, for wildflowers are short-lived, and one species quickly gives way to another as the seasons progress. Should you miss seeing a particular favorite, you could still find it by traveling north, where the seasons arrive later. On the other hand, if you go south, you can get a jump on the seasons and catch some flowers early.

Bear in mind that the long bloom times listed for each flower in this book cover latitudes from south to north. You must discover for yourself exactly when each wildflower opens where you live. Wildflowers appear unexpectedly and disappear quickly. So be alert!

SKUNK CABBAGE
Symplocarpus foetidus

Can you believe that I found this swamp-loving plant blooming in early March, when snow was still on the ground? I have since learned that such a find is to be expected. March is the month when most skunk cabbages come into flower. In some places, large stands of it are already in bloom in February.

Skunk cabbage is well named. When bruised, it gives off a disgusting odor, like that of a dead animal. The horrible smell attracts early hatches of insects, which come and pollinate the plant's tiny yellow blossoms. Look closely inside the curled leaflike spathe and you will see a round spadix covered with tiny flowers. These flowers resemble the heads of fancy stud pins that have been pushed into a pincushion. Stink-loving insects gather pollen from these blossoms and transport them to blossoms on another plant, thus ensuring that seeds will form.

Unlike most plants, skunk cabbage produces its odd-looking flower first, before making leaves. As the weather warms, the flower dies back and is replaced by a clump of bright green leaves. Soon swamp after swamp is turned into a huge cabbage patch.

1

Bloom Time: February, March, April

ROUND-LOBED HEPATICA

Hepatica americana

Hepatica! Whoever thought up such a name for this gorgeous flower? It's from the Greek word for liver. As the story goes, the plant was named for its leaf, which appears to be shaped like a liver. I can't see it myself, but in times past, people seized on any clue that might reveal some use for a flower. A liver-shaped leaf, they believed, meant the plant could cure liver ailments. Modern medicine has dispelled such a notion, but the flower's name has stuck.

Hepatica, like spring beauty and bloodroot, is a flower of early spring. You might even find it blooming under snow cover. How does it withstand the cold weather? Look closely and you will see that it wears a coat of tiny hairs on its stem. These bristles not only protect it from freezing, they also prevent crawling insects from mounting its stem and stealing its nectar. Not all insects are helpful to flowers. Most crawling insects, for example, have bodies too smooth to carry pollen from one plant to another. By contrast, flying insects, such as bumblebees and flies, are often fuzzy creatures. When they alight on a hepatica blossom, their hairy bodies pick up and hold pollen grains, which they then airlift to the next hepatica blossom they visit. By this means, the male pollen from one flower is delivered to the female ovules in another flower, and seeds are formed.

Hepatica comes in three colors: lavender, blue, and white.

Bloom Time: March, April

Round-Lobed Hepatica

Carolina Spring Beauty

CAROLINA SPRING BEAUTY
Claytonia caroliniana

As the name suggests, spring beauties come up early, when the ground is still moist from melted snow and the trees have not yet leafed out. Although they grow in patches, they are easily overlooked. In fact, I would have walked right past the ones shown here had my husband not called my attention to them.

This dainty flower should not be missed. Its soft rose-colored petals are accented with darker stripes and call to mind a piece of peppermint candy. You would think that such a pretty flower would advertise its presence. Spring beauties, however, do just the opposite. Besides being tiny, they close up on overcast days, which makes them even harder to find. On the other hand, they can't resist strong light. As soon as the sun comes out, they unfurl.

A spring beauty flower lasts only three days, but new ones continue to open throughout the month of April or until surrounding trees have grown a leaf canopy that puts them in the shade. Then they shut down for good.

Look for spring beauties in damp woods or near streambeds. The weather may be chilly, but finding one of these flowers is well worth the effort.

Bloom Time: March, April, May

BLOODROOT

Sanguinaria canadensis

The flower of the bloodroot plant is so delicate that even a light breeze can cause its spotless petals to fall off the very day they open. For this reason, I had difficulty finding a perfect blossom to photograph. The slightest brush by a leaf or an insect can cause one or two petals to drop. Needless to say, this exquisite flower cannot be successfully picked.

In its woodland setting, however, bloodroot is a real find. Cloaked by a wraparound leaf, it is an enchanting flower. It is also of historical interest.

The orange sap that runs through its juicy stem creates a permanent stain, and Indians once used this color to paint their faces and dye their baskets.

The fruit of a bloodroot flower looks like a small cigar and is filled with tiny ($\frac{1}{8}$-inch-long) seeds, each one capped with a wee crest. Ants carry away these seeds, gripping them by their minuscule crests, the part they later eat. Thanks to these ant helpers, the seeds of the bloodroot are introduced to new sites, where they sprout the following spring.

Bloom Time: March, April, May

TRAILING ARBUTUS

Epigaea repens

A trailing arbutus plant is hard to find. Besides being rare, it hides under dead leaves, which protect it from April snow. If you brush aside the litter, however, you will uncover the trailing arbutus's leathery foliage, which remains green all winter.

But even after uncovering this plant, you might overlook its tiny pale pink blossoms, which lie hidden within the plant's thick leaves. Not many pollinating insects would find their way to such inconspicuous blooms were it not for the fact that this plant has come up with a special means of attracting them. Perfume! Trailing arbutus exudes a delicious scent that insects like. So do people. In fact, your own nose may help guide you to this shy flower.

Whoever named this species was only half right. It is a trailing plant and cannot stand erect. But arbutus? Arbutus is Latin for strawberry tree, and in no way does this flower resemble a strawberry. Moreover, strawberries do not grow on trees!

In parts of New England, the trailing arbutus is known by a more suitable name. According to legend, it was the first flower the Pilgrims saw upon landing in America, and they called it mayflower for the ship that had brought them here.

Bloom Time: February, March, April

DUTCHMAN'S BREECHES

Dicentra cucullaria

When you look at this flower, do you see several pairs of trousers hanging upside down? Most people do. Dutchman's breeches is a name you'll have an easy time remembering. Bees, however, have no easy time entering this oddly shaped flower. Its yellow-tinged opening is too tight for them to squeeze through. How, then, do they obtain nectar? And if they can't enter, how does the flower spread and receive pollen?

For a long time, botanists believed that the Dutchman's breeches' flower was self-pollinating. To prove this theory, they covered a wide patch of blossoms with sheer gauze that could not be penetrated by even the tiniest midge. The outcome surprised them. Not a single blossom made seeds. The flowers were dependent on insect carriers, after all!

From then on, botanists paid closer attention and observed that a special bumblebee with an unusually long proboscis was able to insert its needlelike tongue into the breeches' tightly closed waist and delve deep inside the flower's "pants' legs" to where nectar is stored. As it darted from flower to flower, the bumblebee's tongue picked up and dropped off load after load of sticky pollen. The botanists saw something else, too. Another smaller type of bee often bit open the breeches' toes and helped itself to free nectar. In so doing, it robbed the flower, which got no service in return for the feast it provided.

Bloom Time: April, May

PURPLE TRILLIUM

Trillium erectum

Here's another flower that uses odor to attract insect helpers. This one, however, is a real stinker. It creates a stench like spoiled meat. As a result, big green flesh flies, in search of dead animals to feed on, are fooled into landing on it. There they become dusted with pollen, which falls into the next purple trillium that tricks them into making a landing.

Flesh flies are not the only living things to be duped by this plant. In times past, people believed that the shape, color, and scent of a plant revealed its use. Because purple trillium smells like rotten meat, it was once used to treat gangrene, a deadly condition in which a part of the human body decays. But it didn't work. Today we no longer rely on such guesswork. Instead, biochemists analyze flowering plants in laboratories and run tests to learn which ones really do have the power to heal.

In some parts of the country, purple trillium is called stinking Benjamin. In other places, it is known as wake-robin. Personally, I prefer to call it purple trillium. "Tri" means three, and this flower has three petals, three sepals, and three leaves.

Bloom Time: April, May, June

MARSH MARIGOLD

Caltha palustris

What a bright splash of yellow the marsh marigold brings to the dark swamps and shadowy brooks where it grows! Its gleaming blossoms enliven these sunless places, which probably accounts for its name—marigold. However, it is not related to the garden flower of the same name. It is, in fact, an oversize, water-loving buttercup.

Like all buttercups, the marsh marigold has a rather primitive design. To begin with, it lacks real petals. What appear to be petals are actually the flower's sepals, waxy and yellow though they be. In most flowers, sepals are green and leaflike and lie beneath the petals, supporting them.

The marsh marigold's reproductive system is also simple. Its blossom contains both male and female parts. These are clearly visible in the photograph. The greenish stems in the center disk are female organs, called pistils, and they contain the ovules, or eggs. The shorter stems that surround these female pistils are the flower's male organs, called stamens. These stamens contain sperm, called pollen.

For any flower to make seeds, male pollen must enter a female pistil—preferably one on a different blossom. Sometimes the male and female parts of the same blossom do mate, but their offspring are less healthy, less productive, and less able to adapt to change than plants born of two parents.

Bloom Time: April, May, June

COMMON BLUE VIOLET

Viola papilionacea

Just because a flower is called violet doesn't mean it comes in only that color. There are five hundred species of violets worldwide. Most are blue or purple, but others are white, yellow, pink, red, and even green. In the United States alone, there are more than one hundred species.

The violet is a highly successful flower, and those who speak of it as being "shrinking" don't know what they're talking about. Uproot an unwanted patch of them from your garden and they'll come back with a vengeance. The violet owes its success to the fact that it has three ways to reproduce. Its familiar blossom is sweet smelling and brightly colored, characteristics that attract pollen-bearing insects to come and fertilize its ovules (eggs). At the same time, the plant produces a second flower, an inconspicuous bud that never opens and is seldom noticed by man or bee. It doesn't need to attract attention, for it fertilizes itself! The violet's third method of reproduction is to send up shoots from its vast root system. One sprawling root may give rise to many, many clones.

Here's a wildflower you can pick without endangering it. Violets have even withstood a time when they were used for food. During the sixteenth century, they were put into soup, candied, and served as garnishes. Pick them, wear them, cook them, eat them, enjoy them. Violets will live on.

Bloom Time: March, April, May, June

JACK-IN-THE-PULPIT

Arisaema triphyllum

This flower recalls my childhood flights of fancy about fairies. I pictured them gathered around preacher Jack, listening to his sermons. What I didn't know was that my imaginary fairies were sometimes listening to preacher Jill, for this plant comes in two forms: one male, the other female. To further confuse matters, a plant that is Jack one year may turn into Jill the next.

Both forms bear tiny blossoms on their columns (called spadixes). The blossoms on male plants are situated near the top of the column and contain pollen-bearing stamens but no egg-producing pistils. The blossoms on female plants are situated near the bottom of the column and contain

egg-producing pistils but no pollen-bearing stamens.

In the majority of wildflower species, both male and female parts occur side by side on the same blossom. Why, then, does the jack-in-the-pulpit produce two kinds of plants, one male and the other female? It does so to ensure that self-fertilization, which results in inferior offspring, can never take place.

In the fall, only the jill-in-the-pulpit produces brilliant red berries. Although poisonous, Indians knew how to get around this problem by long cooking. They also served the taproot as a vegetable, which accounts for the plant's other name: Indian turnip.

Bloom Time: April, May, June

WILD GERANIUM

Geranium maculatum

The wild geranium doesn't look at all like the bright red domesticated geraniums you see in window boxes. Nevertheless, it is a distant cousin of that plant. Both belong to the geranium family, which numbers some eight hundred species.

One feature that all these related species have in common is a pistil that becomes elongated when the plant goes to seed. The botanist who named the family must have thought these pistils resembled cranes' beaks. Geranium is from the Greek word for crane.

It was a geranium that caught the attention of a German botanist in 1782 and led to an important discovery. Until then, people assumed that every flower shed its own male pollen onto its own female part and thus pollinated itself. Christian Sprengel, however, noticed that the geranium's male stamens were positioned too low to drop pollen into the tall female pistils that were located on the same blossom. This arrangement, he theorized, actually *prevented* the flower from pollinizing itself. Upon further observation, he noticed that many bees were buzzing about the flower, picking up and dropping off pollen as they flitted from one blossom to another. Thus he discovered how flowers, with the aid of insects, exchange genetic material. Christian Sprengel's findings revolutionized the thinking of all botanists.

Bloom Time: April, May, June

PINK LADY'S SLIPPER

Cypripedium acaule

Everybody loves the pink lady's slipper. The trouble is, it's being loved to death. Whereas a hundred years ago the species was common, today count yourself lucky if you come across even one of these gorgeous orchids.

It is not just flower pickers who are to blame for this plant's disappearance. Expert gardeners cannot resist the urge to dig up such a beauty and transplant it into their gardens, where it almost certainly will die. The better the gardener, the more likely it is that he or she will view the pink lady's slipper as a challenge, an opportunity to succeed at growing it where others have failed. The pink lady's slipper's root system, however, is extremely fragile and may extend a foot or two around the plant. Moreover, to survive, these delicate roots must live in the company of a rare underground fungus. Even the plant's tiny seeds, no bigger than dust specks, need to be infected by this beneficial fungus or they won't germinate. How many gardeners can provide such special conditions?

This flower faces other threats, too. Every day more of its wild habitats are being logged, converted to agricultural use, or developed for housing. It takes years for a pink lady's slipper to mature and begin making seeds. It cannot keep up with the earthmoving machines.

So love it—and leave it! And tell your friends to do the same.

25

Bloom Time: May, June

COLUMBINE

Aquilegia canadensis

Nature must have been in a whimsical mood when she created columbine. Its blossom droops like a bell, and its yellow stamens and pistils hang down like a bell's clapper. Moreover, each of its five petals is rolled into a long cone and sealed at the tip. It is in these deep tips that nectar is stored, an arrangement that discourages insect pollinators from seeking it. Few will venture up the narrow, dead-end chambers to obtain the sweet liquid.

So what's going on here? Doesn't this flower welcome helpers? The answer is yes—but not *insect* helpers. Columbine is a bird flower, designed to attract hummingbirds. Columbine is red. Hummingbirds like the color red. Columbine's petals are shaped into long cones. The long beaks of hummingbirds fit neatly into these cones. Columbine has no odor. Hummingbirds have no sense of smell. Columbine's scrolled-up petals do not offer insects a landing platform. Hummingbirds need not land to feed. They extract nectar while hovering in midair.

Why did columbine specialize in attracting hummingbirds?

The hummingbird is an active pollinator, for it must consume half its weight in nectar every day. It is also selective. It searches for red tubular flowers and bypasses blossoms that are colored or shaped differently. Therefore, the pollen it picks up from one columbine has an excellent chance of being delivered to a right address—another correctly color-coded columbine flower!

Bloom Time: April, May, June, July

BLUE-EYED GRASS

Sisyrinchium atlanticum

Despite its name, blue-eyed grass is not a grass at all but a member of the iris family. Nor is it always blue. A few of the nine species in our country are white or purple. The flower's center, however, is always golden yellow. Nevertheless, the plant is well named, for its blossom appears to be perched on the very tip of a blade of grass. Moreover, its long stem is flat and grasslike, and it thrives in grassy plots. Where you see one, you will find many others, standing up like jeweled hatpins amidst the greenery.

Although blue-eyed grass enjoys a long season, each blossom lasts but a day, opening its cheery face to the sun in the morning and shutting down for good in the late afternoon. Don't despair, however, if you come upon a patch of these flowers that have withered on the stem. New ones will likely come into bloom the following morning, and continue to do so on a daily basis well into summer.

In spring, blue-eyed grass likes to get its feet wet. In summer, it prefers dry soil. Look for it beside streams that flood their banks in May but run dry by July.

Bloom Time: May, June, July

CANADA LILY
Lilium canadense
WOOD LILY
Lilium philadelphicum

The Canada lily and the wood lily are closely related and have much in common. For example, they grow from bulbs, they have leaves arranged in whorls around their stems, and their petals and sepals are spotted. They differ in that each has discovered its own solution to the problem of rainfall.

Although every plant needs water to live, too much pelting rain can fill a cone-shaped flower and damage its pollen. The Canada lily (right) prevents this from happening by hanging its head. Raindrops run off its umbrellalike petals. The wood lily (left) hit on a different solution to the same problem. Since its blossom faces upward, it could become waterlogged—were it not for the fact that its petals are open at the base. The gaps that exist between the petals allow rain to drain out as fast as it enters the blossom.

Bloom Time: Canada lily—June, July, August; Wood lily—June, July

PASTURE ROSE

Rosa carolina

Don't pick me," says the pasture rose. Not with words, of course. This wild rose speaks with its thorns, which can inflict nasty stab wounds in any tender hand that grasps them.

But didn't wild roses have thorns long before people were around? What was the purpose of thorns in the first place?

No doubt these sharp weapons evolved as a defense against early animals that fed on the plant. Today, thanks to thorns, the wild rose can still defend itself from hungry deer, antelope, cattle, and goats, and we are the better for it. Was there ever a flower more loved?

It is paradoxical that a plant designed to repel browsing animals also produces a tempting morsel meant to attract other hungry creatures. Birds, for example, pluck and eat the fruit of the wild rose, called a rose hip, which is very nutritious and full of vitamin C. In so doing, they act as seed dispensers, for the tasty rose hip is packed with indigestible seeds. The many birds and animals that feed on rose hips pass these hard seeds in their feces, and so spread wild roses about.

Rose hips are used by people, too. They are brewed into a tea that, some say, can cure a cold.

Bloom Time: June, July

Pasture Rose

Orange Hawkweed

ORANGE HAWKWEED

Hieracium aurantiacum

Wildflowers are rarely orange in color, but here is one that is. Orange hawkweed is also called devil's paintbrush, and you can probably guess why. Like many other introduced plants, it competes with native wildflowers and sometimes invades farmers' fields and displaces their crops. At the same time, a field of orange hawkweeds creates a striking scene, especially where they grow alongside king devils (another hawkweed). These two close relatives are often found together.

Except for color, a yellow king devil (above) and an orange hawkweed (right) are hard to tell apart. Both have blossoms shaped like the dandelion's, and both have stems covered with bristly hairs. These hairs are tipped with glands, which produce a sticky substance that entangles any walking insect that tries to mount their stems. Hawkweeds have evolved this strategy to protect their precious nectar bait from being wasted on slow-moving, smooth-bodied beetles or ants. Only airborne pollinators, such as speedy bees, are welcome. When these winged insects take off, a big load of pollen will be stuck to their fuzzy bodies.

Hawkweeds are so named because of an old belief that hawks would occasionally eat them to improve their vision.

Bloom Time: June, July, August

DANDELION
Taraxacum officinale

Not all wildflowers are hard to find. Dandelions crop up just about everywhere, including places where they are not loved. People who want their lawns to be solid green mats of grass do not welcome this cheery yellow invader. Getting rid of it, however, can be difficult. The dandelion's flower ripens into a fluff ball of lightweight seeds that scatter in the breeze. Blow on one of these feathery globes, and chances are you will seed your neighbor's lawn with unwanted dandelions. Still, it is a pretty sight to watch the fluff float away, and children, in particular, like to make it happen.

People are of different minds about this wildflower. While lawnkeepers perceive it as a noxious weed, other folks enjoy eating its leaves, which can be tossed into a salad or cooked and used as a vegetable.

The dandelion has other uses, too. Children yellow their chins with its sticky pollen. Many people like the look of a field that is studded with them. As for me, I fancy the flower's name. Does it mean dandy lion? I used to think so. Now I have learned that it comes from the French "dent de lion," meaning "tooth of the lion." Its jagged leaves certainly do resemble the tearing teeth of a cat. Still, "dandy lion" is the name I like for this golden flower that creeps into our yards and lies about in the grass.

Bloom Time: March, April, May, June, July, August, September

Dandelion gone to seed

Red Clover

RED CLOVER

Trifolium pratense

Farmers love red clover. They use it as forage to feed their cows and horses and sheep and goats. They even use it to feed their soil. Did you know that soil needs to be fed from time to time?

It works like this: Food crops, such as corn or potatoes or carrots, require nitrogen in order to grow, and they obtain this essential ingredient from healthy soil. But a farmer's land can become depleted of nitrogen after years of use. To replenish it, a farmer must rest the land, or better still, plant a crop of red clover on it. The roots of red clover contain tiny nodules that capture and store nitrogen. When the red clover is harvested, stored nitrogen in the remaining roots is released and nourishes the soil.

This kind of intelligent farming is called crop rotation, and it pays off in two ways. In late summer, the farmer can harvest his red clover and use it to feed his livestock all winter. Then in spring, he can plant his refreshed field with beans, potatoes, or corn and expect a bumper crop.

Red clover is not native to North America. It was brought here from Europe by early farmers who understood its practical uses. Since then it has spread across the entire country and can be found in old fields, along roadsides, and perhaps on your lawn. I'm sure you will have no difficulty recognizing it.

Bloom Time: May, June, July, August, September

CHICORY

Cichorium intybus

Blue is the color of the chicory's flower, except in those few instances when a plant produces a pink or a white blossom. I have never seen one that is pink or white, or if I have, I didn't know what it was. To me, blue is the right color for the chicory's flower. Like a piece of sky that has dropped onto some desolate place, this flower brightens the view. I once tried moving one to better conditions, but without success. Chicory likes a cheerless, dusty, dredged-up road shoulder.

Like so many other roadside wildflowers, this flower was brought here from abroad. It does not venture into woods or meadow or marsh, where our native plants are so well adapted to survive. It could not compete with such long-entrenched residents. Therefore, it has taken to the road, so to speak, and we are the better for it. Chicory and Queen Anne's lace and oxeye daisies are a kind of highway beautification committee. They certainly make a long car trip less dreary.

Chicory has practical uses, too. Its roots can be ground up, roasted, and added to coffee. In Europe, the plant is cultivated for this very purpose, and millions of pounds of the packaged grounds are sold to the United States each year.

Look for chicory on a sunny morning. Its blossoms close when the sun is low or when there is cloud cover.

45

Bloom Time: June, July, August, September, October

Chicory

Toadflax

TOADFLAX

Linaria vulgaris

Flowers do the darnedest things. On the previous page you can see a toadflax that has barred a weevil from entering its blossom. The weevil is not big enough or strong enough to pry open the blossom's tightly closed lips (the upper lip is light yellow and the lower lip is deep yellow), and so the weevil has turned away and will have to seek nectar elsewhere.

Why would a flower not admit an insect into its blossom? Doesn't the toadflax need a porter to deliver its pollen from one blossom to another?

Yes, it does, but it doesn't need such a tiny insect, one that is so smooth. Very little pollen, if any, would stick to the weevil's slick body. So the toadflax has set its jaws firmly against all but the biggest, fuzziest, and fastest insects, like the bee on the facing page. Unlike the weevil, the bee is quite capable of prying apart the flower's tight lips and wedging itself inside.

Some people call this flower butter-and-eggs, and I think that is quite a good name for it. Its light shade of yellow suggests butter; its deeper shade of yellow suggests an egg yolk. The deep shade actually serves a purpose. It guides the bee to the mouth of the flower and is called a honey path.

Bloom Time: June, July, August, September, October

PURPLE LOOSESTRIFE

Lythrum salicaria

Purple loosestrife is usually seen from afar, growing in masses that fill entire swamps or covering marshy meadows too wet for walking. The effect is radiant. Often you will see cars parked along a highway so that their occupants can take in the sight.

Once again, we have Europe to thank (or blame) for this imported plant. Gorgeous as it is, purple loosestrife has crowded out many of our own aquatic species. Our native yellow loosestrife, also called swamp candle, has difficulty competing with this aggressive plant, as does our native cattail (seen in the lower right-hand corner of the picture). Since these homegrown aquatics provide habitat and food for marsh birds and muskrats, many environmentalists do not cheer the advance of purple loosestrife across acres and acres of wetlands.

Its blossoms, however, are of special interest to botanists. They occur in three forms, which can be sorted out according to the lengths of their pistils and stamens. As a result of these varying lengths, each form can accept pollen only from a blossom that is unlike itself.

Sadly, there is little likelihood that our swamps and marhses will ever be restored to their original condition. Nevertheless, concerned people are trying to come up with some safe way to halt the further spread of this beautiful but unwelcome flower.

Bloom Time: June, July, August, September

Purple Loosestrife

Queen Anne's Lace

QUEEN ANNE'S LACE

Daucus carota

Queen Anne's lace is the perfect name for this delicate flower. Actually, it isn't just one flower. Look closely and you will see that several clusters of tiny florets form its intricate lacy pattern. When used in a mixed bouquet, Queen Anne's lace sets off larger, more showy blossoms. And, yes, you may pick this wildflower. It is in no danger of disappearing.

Farmers wish that it would. With the same intensity that they love red clover, they dislike Queen Anne's lace. It invades their fields and, if not pulled up, will take over, sapping their crops of nutrition and taking up valuable space.

Still, it has its admirers. It adds beauty to roadways, especially where it grows alongside more colorful wildflowers. It also deserves our thanks for giving rise to the carrot. In fact, its first-year taproot is a carrot. Of course, over many centuries of domestication, the carrots we grow and eat today have been greatly improved. If, however, you should ever find yourself lost and hungry, you might try eating this wild root.

As Queen Anne's lace ages and begins to wither, its flat clusters curl up around the edges, and the fading blossom takes the shape of a bird's nest. In some parts of the country, the common name for this plant is bird's nest.

Bloom Time: May, June, July, August, September, October

OXEYE DAISY

Chrysanthemum leucanthemum

The oxeye daisy is native to the British Isles and was brought to America by colonists. They probably wanted their new country to look like the homeland they had left, and they succeeded. This import has spread across the entire continent, and today just about every American is familiar with it.

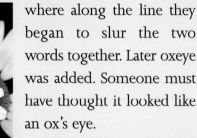

Here is another wildflower that it's okay to pick, for it isn't in any danger of disappearing. Moreover, dairy farmers will be thankful if you remove it from their fields, because when cows eat it, they produce odd-tasting milk.

How did the daisy get its name?

Long ago it was called day's eye, but people from different parts of England spoke in dialects, and somewhere along the line they began to slur the two words together. Later oxeye was added. Someone must have thought it looked like an ox's eye.

You've probably played "She loves me, she loves me not" with a daisy. The outcome of that game depends on whether the flower you are plucking has an odd number or an even number of rays. (What appear to be petals are actually called rays in this flower.) Since each daisy varies in the number of rays it produces, the game isn't rigged!

Bloom Time: June, July, August

NIGHTSHADE

Solanum dulcamara

A flower with the name night-shade probably doesn't have many friends and admirers, and that's too bad. It is strikingly beautiful. Its sweptback petals and beaklike center are so graceful that they appear to be the work of a jeweler. I, for one, would like to wear a pair of nightshade-designed pendants in my ears.

Even the fruit of this vine is attractive, but that can be a problem. The shiny berries, so appealing to the eye, are poisonous. Are they deadly? They certainly can cause illness, but perhaps they are not deadly for everyone. At least some people must have survived a taste test long enough to write about the experience. In old books night-shade has been described as having a bitter first taste, followed by a sweet aftertaste. Moreover, records in England describe how its berries were once used to ward off witchcraft. Obviously, people must have eaten them.

Would I sample one?

Absolutely not! There are, however, several close relatives of night-shade whose fruit I mightily enjoy. These are: the potato, the eggplant, the green pepper, and especially the tomato.

Bloom Time: May, June, July, August, September

SLENDER DAYFLOWER

Commelina erecta

The dayflower blooms for just one day. In that short time, it must be noticed and visited by a pollinator, or it will not make seeds. Therefore, it puts on a lovely display of color to advertise its free nectar. The two largest of its three petals are a heavenly shade of blue and stand up like Mickey Mouse ears. Its third petal is small and obscure and colorless, for the plant wastes no pigment on it. It has a more important flourish to make. From the center of its blossom, six golden-yellow long-stemmed stamens grow up and wave like tiny flags, beckoning every passing insect to drop in for a drink of nectar. Now, what thirsty

insect could resist such an invitation?

As it happens, the blossom in the picture to the left has already hosted a pollinator. Some insect has visited it and deposited grains of pollen gathered from another dayflower onto its female pistil tips. These pistil tips, or stigmas, appear to be clutching the precious pollen. In actual fact, the pistil tips are so sticky there is little chance that the pollen could blow away.

The dayflower is a good example of how a flower's design can prevent self-pollination. Any pollen grains that might be shed by this blossom's own stamens cannot possibly fall into its own pistils. As you can see, its pistils are too tall.

Bloom Time: July, August, September, October

CARDINAL FLOWER
Lobelia cardinalis

When I look at the gorgeous blossom of the cardinal flower, I see an exotic bird with a long neck, a white head, two red wings, and three red feathers in its tail. It is the flower I most hope to find when I walk in a wild place. And when I do, it is like coming upon a precious jewel.

The cardinal flower blossom is a complicated affair. The white part, which I have described as looking like a bird's head, is actually called a beard. It is this beard that brushes pollen onto the heads of hummingbirds, the flower's chief pollinators. These tiny birds are irresistibly drawn to the color red, and so the cardinal flower has dressed itself in a shade unmatched by any other flower. The red of its petals is so intense that it almost seems to vibrate. Such a color is all the more remarkable when you consider that the cardinal flower belongs to the bluebell family, which specializes in blue, white, and lavender blossoms.

The cardinal flower has been admired for a long, long time. French explorers to the New World were awed by it and carried it back to Paris. Viewers there compared it to the red robes worn by Roman Catholic cardinals. And that's how the cardinal flower got its name.

Bloom Time: July, August, September

Cardinal Flower

Indian Blanket

INDIAN BLANKET
Gaillardia pulchella

Have you ever seen woven Indian blankets that consist of alternating bands of red and yellow? Perhaps the weavers were inspired by this flower. It wouldn't be surprising, for Native Americans get many of their design ideas from nature.

A two-tone flower is always striking, especially when many bloom together. The contrasting colors create the effect of a mixed bouquet. In the Great Plains states, where Indian blankets grow to be four feet tall, entire fields are sometimes covered with them, and it is a sight to behold. A smaller variety of the flower grows in the Midwest and the South. The smaller Indian blanket also occurs in the East, although some guidebooks fail to mention this fact.

The Indian blanket has many relatives: black-eyed Susan, oxeye daisy, and the entire aster family, to name a few. All of these flowers are called composite flowers—meaning that a single blossom is actually composed of many, many flowers. So what appears to be just one Indian blanket is, in fact, many. Examine the center of the bloom shown on the previous page and you will discover two distinct types of tiny florets, called disk flowers. More surprising is the fact that the bloom's petals are not petals at all but yet another type of flower, known as ray flowers.

You have to marvel at all the complicated strategies wildflowers have come up with to perpetuate themselves.

Bloom Time: August, September

SWEET GOLDENROD

Solidago odora

There are eighty species of goldenrod in this country, many of which are so alike that they are hard to identify. The one you see here is called sweet goldenrod. It is possible to recognize it by its odor. Its leaves, when crushed, smell like licorice.

Tiny bugs are attracted to goldenrod. They take tiny sips from tiny florets that make up this plant's dense floral clusters. Often a wand of goldenrod will be crawling with insects, all bent on sipping nectar.

The sight of a field of goldenrod in full bloom made me sad when I was a child, for it meant the end of summer. At the same time, I loved the look of this canary-yellow wildflower and wanted to gather big bouquets of it to give to my mother. But this couldn't be.

"Don't bring home any goldenrod," she had warned me. "I'm allergic to it."

Like many people, she mistakenly believed that goldenrod brought on her late-summer hay fever, when what actually caused her misery was ragweed. The two plants come into bloom at the same time, and goldenrod, being the more visible of the two, has long been viewed as the culprit.

Bloom Time: July, August, September

TURTLEHEAD

Chelone glabra

If you've ever looked closely at a turtlehead blossom, you'll probably agree that the flower is perfectly named. It is shaped much like an actual turtle's head. And when the blossom's "mouth" is forced open by a bee, you can see the pink interior, which contains a "tongue." I think it is fitting that this wildflower grows alongside ponds, where turtles often show their heads.

I looked for turtleheads for a long time before I came upon some on a narrow bank beside a brook. After getting good and wet photographing them, I returned home— only to find one growing in my own yard. It had introduced itself to our rock garden, which is watered by a fountain.

Just as the toadflax requires hefty bumblebees to strong-arm their way into its closed blossom, so does the turtlehead. In late summer and early fall, these tight-lipped wildflowers are plentiful, and the services of oversize bumblebees are in great demand.

Bloom Time: July, August, September

COMMON SKULLCAP
Scutellaria epilobiifolia

The skullcap is an advanced flower that leaves nothing to chance. It has evolved into a shape that guarantees visiting insects will make contact with its stamens and pistil. For instance, one of its lower petals is enlarged to serve as a convenient landing platform. To further aid a prospective pollinator, this platform is marked with dotted lines, which serve as a kind of road map leading to the flower's nectar treat at the very bottom of a long tube. Inside the tube, its female organ, or pistil, is positioned to scoop up any pollen the insect may have brought from another blossom. Its male organs, or stamens, on the other hand, are positioned to dump a load of fresh pollen on the insect's back when it exits.

Like many wildflowers, the skullcap depends on a particular pollinator. Its opening is too small to admit insects larger than honeybees. So honeybees must be attracted. The flower's color succeeds in doing this. Honeybees are drawn to purplish blue, just as hummingbirds favor red. It is no accident, therefore, that the skullcap is such a luscious color.

Whoever named this wildflower must have thought its top petal looked like a skullcap. I can't see it, but I like the name anyway.

Bloom Time: June, July, August, September

PURPLE CONEFLOWER

Echinacea purpurea

At one time, a great rolling prairie covered much of the middle part of North America. Pioneers who crossed that vast grassland wrote of the difficulty they had pushing their way through it, for in some places the grass stood as tall as a man. Wildflowers also grew there, and these, too, were tall. They had to be, or they would have been put into the shade by the tall grasses. And so they reached for the sunlight and grew to be giants.

The purple coneflower is one of those tall prairie wildflowers. Some grow to be five feet high. Those I have found, however, haven't been that towering, and there is a reason for this. Long ago, the tall-grass prairie that gave rise to this plant was converted into farmland. Today the purple coneflower no longer has to reach so high to obtain its share of sunlight.

The blossom of the purple coneflower is similar in design to that of the oxeye daisy, except that its rays are not stiff but sweptback, suggesting a bird in flight. Also, its center disk is spiny, like a sea urchin. This accounts for its Greek name, *Echinacea*, which means sea urchin.

Many people use this striking plant in their gardens. Not only does it provide a beautiful backdrop for smaller plantings, it is also a magnet for butterflies. Fortunately, purple coneflower seeds can be ordered through catalogs, making it unnecessary to collect this lovely flower from the wild.

Bloom Time: June, July, August, September, October

Purple Coneflowers

Joe-Pye Weed

JOE-PYE WEED

Eupatorium maculatum

How would you like to have a flower named after you? That happened to an American Indian named Joe Pye who lived during colonial times. Joe Pye knew a lot about plants. He even knew how to use wildflowers to cure illnesses.

In those days, people did not understand that they should take precautions to prevent the spread of disease; moreover, antibiotics had not yet been discovered. As a result, when someone contracted an infectious disease, it spread rapidly.

Once when a typhus epidemic struck a New England village, the residents sought help from Joe Pye, who responded by bringing the ailing people big bunches of tall flowers. Now, those flowers were not meant to cheer the sick. Joe Pye brought them to heal his patients. How he prepared the flowers—whether he used the leaves, the roots, or the blossoms—is not known, but as the story goes, whatever he did worked. The people got well. And from that day forward, this tall flower has been called Joe-Pye weed.

Curing the sick is not the only thing this plant is good for. It is an important food for monarch butterflies. They sip it before embarking on their two-thousand-mile flight to Mexico, where they spend the winter.

Bloom Time: July, August, September

NODDING LADIES' TRESSES

Spiranthes cernua

I found this native orchid growing in a soggy ditch, and thinking I could improve its lot, I moved it to a better location. What a mistake! It did not survive.

Orchids are fussy. This one's root system is so fragile that it breaks apart when handled. Moreover, like the pink lady's slipper, this orchid lives in partnership with a particular underground fungus that helps it obtain nourishment from the soil. When separated from this fungus, it starves.

I didn't know these facts when I tried to transplant it. Now I do, and I will never again move any orchid. What's more, I tell everybody who'll listen to enjoy this family of flowers where they grow.

Although the nodding ladies' tresses is small and inconspicuous, it is a real find, for close examination will reveal how exquisite it is. I used a close-up lens to take this photograph so you can see how the plant's tiny blossoms spiral up an erect stem and resemble a braid. That accounts for the species name. Tresses is an old-fashioned word for long locks of hair.

Most orchids live in the tropics. We're lucky for the few we have in our country. Several varieties of ladies' tresses grow in our eastern states. Most of these are tiny, but a southern species, called fragrant ladies' tresses, sometimes grows to be three feet tall.

Bloom Time: September, October

NEW YORK IRONWEED
Vernonia noveboracensis

Nature never stops experimenting. This time, she's created a flower that appears to be made of curly ribbons.

Ironweed grows in moist lowlands and is tall. The one I photographed towered over my head. I made a point to return and measure it and found it to be nine feet high.

Imagine wandering through a forest of New York ironweeds, which often grow in large stands. In such a place, you would certainly find hummingbirds, for they are attracted to the ironweed's reddish-purple blossoms. In fact, three of these pollinators hovered over my head while I was shooting pictures. As they probed for hidden nectar, their long beaks easily penetrated the blossoms' curly heads.

How it happened that the name New York was attached to this plant is hard to fathom, since New York ironweed grows in many states. Perhaps someone used the label "New York" to distinguish it from another variety of ironweed that also grows in New York and elsewhere—namely, tall ironweed. As for the name ironweed, it suits the plant, whose stem is tough and resembles the trunk of a young tree.

In times past, this giant plant was thought to cure stomach ailments. Whether or not it does, ironweed is a valuable fall flower. It provides hummingbirds with a source of nourishment shortly before they begin their long migration south for the winter.

Bloom Time: August, September, October

New York Ironweed

Closed Gentian

CLOSED GENTIAN

Gentiana andrewsii

Do you think that what you see here are flower buds? Well, don't hold your breath waiting for them to open, because they never will. This plant is in full flower right now.

How is that possible? How does such a wildflower exchange pollen with another of its kind when its stamens and pistils are so tightly enclosed by its petals?

Many botanists have asked the same question, and for a long time they concluded that the closed gentian was self-pollinating. Then somebody observed a large bumblebee forcing apart the flower's closed petals and squeezing into its budlike blossom. Once inside, the bee used its long tongue to reach the nectar stored at the base of the flower. When the bee backed out, it was showered with pollen, which it delivered to the next closed gentian it visited. So much for the self-pollination theory.

This autumn flower was loved by one of our great poets, Emily Dickinson. She wrote:

> God made a little gentian:
> It tried to be a rose
> And failed, and all the summer laughed.
> But just before the snows
> There came a purple creature
> That ravished all the hill;
> And summer hid her forehead,
> And mockery was still.

Many states list this species as threatened, so look for it, enjoy it, and leave it alone.

Bloom Time: August, September, October

NEW ENGLAND ASTER
Aster novae-angliae

What flower family could be more American than the aster? It arose on this continent long, long ago, and over the course of time it successfully spawned 120 variations in shades of blue, purple, white, and pink. These differing species are also distinguished by blossom size, leaf shape, and plant height.

As you can see, the one that I have included here is deep violet and so adds another hue to the autumn spectacle of orange, red, and yellow foliage. This special color attracts butterflies and what few drowsy bees are still around and foraging. Since pollinating insects are scarce in fall, the aster must be patient—its blooms must last a long time. It must also take extra precaution to protect its precious nectar bait from feeders ill-equipped to transport pollen. That's why this flower has evolved hairy stems. Any ground insect that attempts to climb it will become entangled in the bristles. As a second barrier against wingless, smooth-backed insects, the New England aster produces many leaves that hug its stems.

Although it is named New England aster, this flower has a range that extends as far west as Colorado and as far south as North Carolina. It is also cultivated in backyard gardens by aster-loving people.

Fall-blooming asters are as precious as the last rose of summer. They stay around until wintry weather interrupts the annual cycle of wild flowering, which will again resume in the spring.

Bloom Time: August, September, October, November

FURTHER READING

Art, Henry W. *A Garden of Wildflowers: 101 Native Species and How to Grow Them.* Pownal, Vermont: Storey Communications Inc., 1986.

Bernhardt, Peter. *Wily Violets and Underground Orchids: Revelations of a Botanist.* New York: William Morrow, 1980.

Dana, Mrs. William Starr. *How to Know the Wildflowers.* Boston: Houghton Mifflin, 1989.

Dowden, Anne Ophelia. *The Secret Life of the Flowers.* New York: Odyssey Press, 1964.

————. *Wild Green Things in the City.* New York: Thomas Y. Crowell, 1972.

Neiring, William A., and Nancy C. Olmstead. *National Audubon Society Field Guide to North American Wildflowers.* New York: Alfred A. Knopf, 1997.

Peterson, Roger Tory, and Margaret McKenny. *A Field Guide to Wildflowers of Northeastern and North-Central North America.* Boston: Houghton Mifflin, 1968.